Dedication

to MR. D &
OUR MERMAIDS &
OUR PROMISE to create
a REMARKABLE LIFE ♥

Philanthropy is in ACTION

A PORTION of PROFITS
FROM EVERY BOOK is
Re-invested iN KIVA

BOOK
deets

© Leonie Dawson International Pty Ltd
BenBella Books, Inc.
10440 N. Central Expressway, Suite 800
Dallas, TX 75231
www.benbellabooks.com
Send feedback to
feedback@benbellabooks.com
ISBN: 9781948836425

Let's get social!

⬜ MYSHINiNGYEAR

f MYSHiNiNGYEAR

↗ MYSHiNiNGYEAR.COM

fB.COM/GROUPS/SHINiNGYEA(

Contents

(i.e., where to find all the goodies!)

It's a table— get it?

MUST-HAVE ITEM

"I've been using the workbooks for a few years now. They've allowed me to achieve some really crazy goals I've set for myself. They are a must-have if you want to create an amazing year."

—Denise Duffield-Thomas, author of *Lucky Bitch*

A GUIDE TO BUILD MY BUSINESS

"Leonie Dawson's workbooks are SO powerful. I have used them every year for the last 8 years. I gush about them all the time. Whatever I put in these workbooks ends up becoming destiny. I cannot recommend them enough."

—Hibiscus Moon, author + crystal expert

HIGHLY RECOMMENDED

"I love these workbooks and have used them for years for my life and business. Whatever I write in there ends up happening. I highly recommend them."

—Nathalie Lussier, entrepreneur, AccessAlly

TRULY TOOK MY BUSINESS TO THE NEXT LEVEL!

"[This] workbook was the swift kick in the butt I needed to start looking at my business for what it really is—a huge source of joy in my life. Since doing the workbook I have tripled my monthly income and found financial freedom in my business!"
—Flora Sage, author, speaker + coach

HELPED ME CREATE AN AUTHENTIC BUSINESS!

"[This] workbook helped me identify what really mattered to me in my business and life, and helped me develop a business that was completely grounded in those values . . . My business brings me joy and I feel set free from what a person in my industry 'should' look like."
—Katie Cowan, Symphony Law's founder, director, chief lawyer

I CANNOT TELL YOU THE IMPACT THAT THE WORKBOOK HAD ON MY BUSINESS!

"Leonie's straight-talking, comprehensible approach to business made it easy for me to take all the steps I had either been avoiding or wasn't even aware I should be taking. Within a month I had not only been brave enough to set income targets for the first time, I had met and overshot them!"
—Kate Beddow, holistic therapist

EASY & POWERFUL WAY TO TRANSFORM!
"Thanks to Leonie's intuitive and business skills I have grown both my business and in my personal life. I feel so much more in tune with my needs and I've gained so much clarity. It is so clear to me now that anything is possible. Let the magic begin!"
—Karina Ladet, intuitive healer

AMAZED AT THE IMPACT IT HAD!
"Wow! I'm a big forward thinker, and straight away this shifted my thinking because first up I had to reflect on the year just past, which was incredibly powerful . . . I ended up purchasing copies for several of my coaching clients so they could enjoy the experience of completing their own workbook too!"
—Belinda Jackson, marketing + business strategist

I WAS BLOWN AWAY!
"To be honest, I was a bit skeptical when I bought the workbook . . . However, I was BLOWN AWAY by the value offered . . . After going through the workbooks, I had a clear plan for achieving both my personal and business goals. I'm now calmer, more focused, and more productive . . . My monthly income has more than doubled!"
—Shay de Silva, fitness coach + founder of Fast Fitness To Go

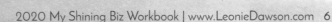

CONGRATULATIONS

YAY!

ON choosing this book. On stepping up to make your **dreams** come true! On saying **YES!** to Being a CONSCIOUS CREATOR of your own Life + Business.

BUSINESS does not have to **BREAK** you, your finances, your work/Life Balance or your spirit. Instead business can be enormously **joyful**, $ **Profitable** + a ➡ force for **good** in the world.

 # What do you need to make that shift happen?

①. Take the vow ⤵

> I, _____,
>   NAME
> do solemnly swear that I am
> committed to my own success. That
> I am 100% responsible for my
> actions and subsequent results. By
> aligning my actions with my intentions,
> I become a Master of My Own
> Destiny.
>
> _____   _____
> SIGNED   DATE

Fill out this WORKBOOK

It is NOT enough to just BUY it & use it as a paper-weight.

You Must actually DO THE THING and...

fill it out!

Set a **deadline**

NOW for when you will completely fill out this WORKBOOK

I will fill out this workbook by

_____
date

3. Schedule in Your GOALS

- LOOK at a calendar for the year ahead + map out some of your BIG GOALS!

- LOOK at your daily + weekly schedule to build in more GOAL-getting time

JUNE 30

"You are the **AVERAGE** of the **5** people you spend your time with. Make them **GOOD** ones!"

—Jim Rohn

4. Surround yourself with MORE goal-getters

join the FaceBook group just for shining Year workbookers!

fb.com/groups/shiningyear

#MYSHININGYEAR

Use & search the books' hashtag on Social Media to find other workbookers!

CREATE a local workbook group!

gRaB the free guide on how to create & Run one at:

myshiningyear.com/groups

SHARE

YOUR WORKBOOK PICS ON SOCIAL MEDIA to FinD OTHER goal - getters

#MYSHININGYEAR

Don't forget to hashtag!

) REGULARLY LOOK at YOUR GOALS!

ARRY this Book
ith You. Make it
og-eaRed & well
LoveD. ♡

use the Monthly
Check-in worksheets
at the end of this
workbook.

The MoRe
You LooK At
YouR GoaLs,
the FasteR they
CoMe tRue!

URRoUnd YouRself
th otheR GoAL-
tteRs. Have
gular workbook
eetups!

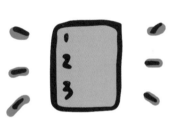

HAve A notecARD
with YouR top
3 goals You ARe
cuRRently working
on. Keep in YouR
wallet oR above
YouR desk.

Create A
Desktop oR
phone wallpapeR
that ReMinds
You of YouR
goals.

Want to be in the top (1%) of achievers?

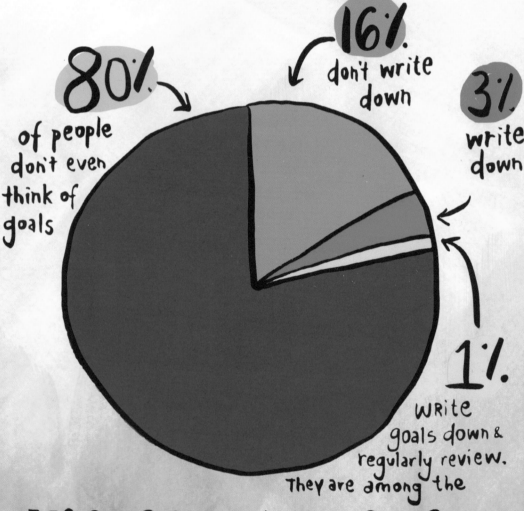

80% of people don't even think of goals

16% don't write down

3% write down

1% write goals down & regularly review. They are among the

HIGHEST ACHIEVERS!

"

A MILLIONAIRE LOOKS at their GOALS ONCE a day...

A BILLIONAIRE LOOKS at their GOALS TWICE a day!

Results

 Increased **income**

 Increased **AuDience**

 Reach your BIZ goals **faster**

 BetteR WORK/LIFE **Balance**

 Increased Self ConfiDence

 MORE **clarity**

 Renewed **PASSION**

INSERT YOUR deaRest wish here

- - - - - - - -

 Have YOUR Best Year Yet in Biz!

DO YOU NEED to fill out this whole book for it to work?

YES

Something is better than NOTHING!
Do what you can or are called to.
The MORE You put in, the MORE You will
get out of it. ♡ YOUR FUTURE
SELF will thank You ♡

Why learn from me?

* International best-selling author
☆ Creator of multiple 7-figure companies
♡ Finalist for Ausmumpreneur of the Year awards + MyBusiness' Business Woman of the Year awards

The
very important

closing
ceremony!

WHY REVIEW the past year?

So often we want to →JUMP→ straight into setting **NEW** goals, dreaming **NEW** dreams before we do the

All-Important Work,

of Reviewing the Past YEAR.

To leap FORWARD into the future we must first:

1. Know where we are Right Now

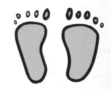

2. Take the time to mine for clarity, insights & Lessons Learned from the past. It is a veritable treasure chest that will make you happier & richer!

But before
we begin
mining for last year's
treasure...
A love
letter for you

Dearest You,

You've been sent here on a mission. A mission to discover every part of yourself. To grow wiser & deeper & more compassionate. To find light in even the darkest cave.

The last year happened to you the way it did for a reason. Even if you're not sure what that reason is yet. Even if it felt hard & unreasonable. It's all taking you where you need to go.

Sometimes we can only learn by going there. You are growing braver, deeper, more precious by the day, by the year.

Let's celebrate & Release the Last Year... Clear the way for Miracles to Come ♥

let's play

WHAT WORKED? WHAT DIDN'T?

WHAT WORKED?

WHAT DIDN'T?

PRODUCTION
MAKING OR SOURCING YOUR PRODUCT/SERVICE

STAFFING
EMPLOYEES + CONTRACTORS

	WHAT WORKED?	WHAT DIDN'T?
TECHNOLOGY + SOFTWARE		
SYSTEMS ORGANIZATION + RECORDKEEPING		

WHAT WORKED?	WHAT DIDN'T?
DAILY WORK ROUTINE	
OFFICE SPACE	

	WHAT WORKED?	**WHAT DIDN'T?**
MARKETING		
CUSTOMER SERVICE		

WHAT WORKED?

WHAT DIDN'T?

CASHFLOW

WORK/LIFE BALANCE

Every twist & turn in life is an opportunity to learn something NEW about YOURSELF. YOUR interests. YOUR talents & how to SET & then ACHIEVE goals

-Jameela Jamil

Let's get our

NUMBERS

on!

Some people call this REPORTING. I call it data that makes you dollars! CLARITY BREEDS ABUNDANCE!

(DEEP BREATH)

Okay, Love.
Are you READY?
It's time to LOOK at
 money!

Now... Before your chest constricts + your
fingers want to flick past this section...
please know you can do this.
We often avoid looking at Real Figures wh
is exactly what is needed to INCREAS
income, decrease expenses + grow prof

Yes, knowing our numbers really (is)
that IMPORTANT + Powerful!

Finances

Income	
Expenses	
PROFIT	

Create a Pie Chart of your expenses & Profit Levels ↪→

income flow

What did you earn each month?

JAN: _____   JULY: _____

FEB: _____   AUG: _____

MAR: _____   SEPT: _____

APR: _____   OCT: _____

MAY: _____   NOV: _____

JUNE: _____   DEC: _____

Sketch a line graph to see the FLOW

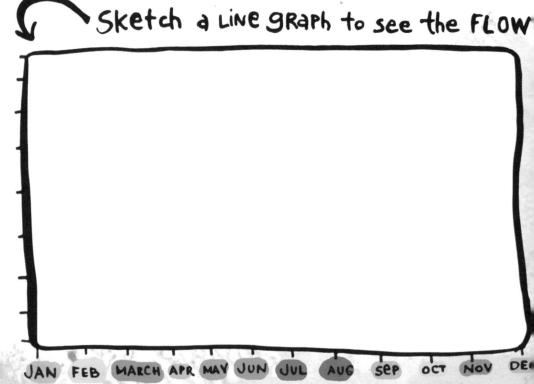

$

JAN FEB MARCH APR MAY JUN JUL AUG SEP OCT NOV DEC

WHAT WERE YOUR BEST-SELLING PRODUCTS/SERVICES LAST YEAR?

OFFERING NAME	HOW MUCH IT MADE
1.	
2.	
3.	
4.	
5.	

Create a **Pie Chart** of how your top offerings SOLD →

HOW MUCH DID YOUR AUDIENCE GROW IN LAST YEAR?

Platform	current #	number grew by...
Mailing list		
FaceBook		
Instagram		
YouTube		

Add your own here!

What insights did you get from your NUMBERS? What do you want to do differently now?

2019 Review

Best Day In Biz:

Worst Day In Biz:

How many holidays you took:

New offerings you Released:

Most Fun:

Best Customer:

Worst Customer:

Best Courses, books + Mentors:

Biggest Revenue In A Day:

UNPLANNED SUCCESSES:

BIGGEST MISTAKES:

WHAT YOU want to do MORE of:

What you want to do LESS of:

What helped Most with stRESS:

HOW DID YOUR BUSINESS PROMOTE + support
diversity + inclusivity?

HOW MUCH YOUR BUSINESS donated to philanthropy:

HOW DID YOUR BUSINESS REDUCE its enviRoNMENtal
iMPACT:

What are your BIZ accomplishments over the past year?
(Fill the page—they can be big or small! They are ALL important!)

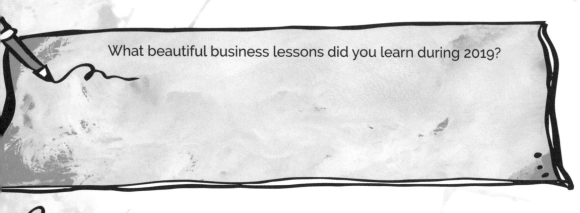

What beautiful business lessons did you learn during 2019?

What were the areas that felt out of whack, hard to follow, or crazy-making in your business this year?
What could be done to change them?

What was the worst thing about your business in 2019?

What did you learn from this?

What was the best thing about your business in 2019?

What did you learn from this?

What do you need to write, journal, or rant about for you to feel clear about 2019 in your business?

GratiTude

A page of gratitude. Draw, write, illustrate, post pictures of
EVERYTHING you are grateful for in your biz from 2019!

COMPLETION CIRCLE

I breathe & give thanks for all that HAS PASSED.

I OPEN up to ALL the beautiful possibilities BLOSSOMING before me.

I Let go & breathe. Releasing all that holds me back FROM MY Magnificence.

I AM safe.
I AM LOVED.
I AM KNOWN.
I have 1000 angels cheering me on.

Place your hand in the circle.

MY SHINING

2020

INVOKING THE YEAR AHEAD

It's TIME to DREAM A NEW DREAM. Time to create a SHINING YEAR for YOU + YOUR WORLD. FIRST comes the THOUGHT. Then comes the WORD. Then the ACTION. That's how CHANGE happens.

ARE YOU READY?

 YES

 No

The New Year stands before us, like a chapter in a book waiting to be written. We can help WRITE THAT STORY by setting goals.

-Melody Beattie

MY SHINING Finances

FinanceS

It's time to cast your mind forward and consider how you want your business finances to look in 2020. How much income would you like to earn? How much of that would be profit? Use the following pages to help you brainstorm these numbers in more detail.

Income	
Expenses	
PROFIT	

★ EXPENSES ★
BUDGETING

It's time to do some estimates of your biz costs. It's OK if this changes over time!

Biz Expense	Estimate
Your Salary	
Staff	
Rent	
Equipment + Supplies	
Software	
Web Design / Hosting	

Add Your Own Here

income POSSIBILITIES

play around with different SALES NUMBERS & PRICES to see what feels like the right fit FOR You.

OFFERING	PRICE	#SOLD	TOTAL
e.g. Artwork prints	$20	100	$2000
GRAND TOTAL			

Do you have the right bookkeeper or accountant to support your business financially?

YES   NO

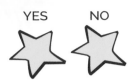

How much do you currently have in business savings?

How much do you need in order to pay tax obligations?

Do you need credit cards or loans for your business to help with cashflow as you grow?

YES   NO

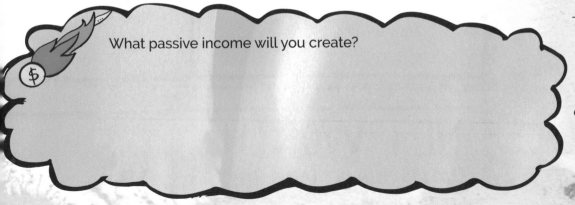

What passive income will you create?

Calculate Your Company's Net Worth

Dearest, please note that this is not for working out your personal net worth. Do that in your Shining Life workbook!

This is for your business as an entity and it's important to start looking at your net worth + the company's net worth as separate.

ADD YOUR OWN HERE

Assets	$ Worth
Equipment	
Stock	
TOTAL ASSETS	

Liabilities	$ Cost
Credit Cards	
Loans	
TOTAL LIABILITIES	

NET WORTH (ASSETS MINUS LIABILITIES)	

Deas to improve finances!

Move to an online accounting system

Use the Monthly Money Making worksheets at end of this book!

Find (or uplevel to) a great Accountant or Bookkeeper

ntinue investing me + Money in ur financial ducation!

Work on your Mindset + Money Blocks

Improve cash flow by improving invoicing, debt collection, terms of payment, etc.

RECOMMENDED RESOURCES FOR MONEY

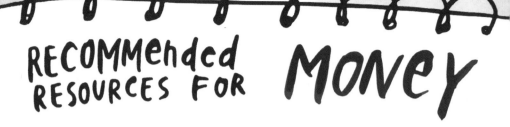

Get RICH LUCKY Bitch — Denise Duffield-Thomas

Secrets of the MILLIONAIRE MIND — T. HARV EKER

The Millionaire Next Door — Thomas J. Stanley

THE Barefoot Investor — S. PAPE

The ONE Minute Millionaire — Allen + Hansen

It's Rising Time! — K. Kiyosaki

Retire Young Retire Rich — R. Kiyosaki

It's NOT ABOUT THE Money — B. Proctor

The RICHEST Man In Babylon — G.S. Clason

Create a **vision** that makes you want to **jump** out of Bed in the **Morning!**

MY Shining Team

Do you have the team you need?   YES   NO

What's working well with your team right now?

What's not working well? How can you improve it?

What roles
do you need to
fill this year?

What additional support do you need from your team?

What is keeping you from growing your team?

Do you have the contractors you need?

YES   NO

What's working well with your contractors right now?

What's not working well? How can you improve it?

Do you have the suppliers you need?

Brainstorm how you could make an even better working relationship with suppliers:

How can you better practice intersectional equality in your business? How can you better educate yourself and your staff to create a concious business?

RECOMMENDED RESOURCES FOR TEAM

Delivering Happiness
· T. HSIEH

The Five DYSFUNCTIONS of A TEAM
P. Lencioni

DaRe to LeaD — Brené Brown

TOP GRADING · Bradford Smart

Peak · chip Conley

NO B.S. Time Management for Entrepreneurs — D. KENNEDY

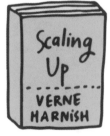
Scaling Up — — — — VERNE HARNISH

The E-MYTH REVISITED M.E. GERBER

HOW THE MiGHTY FALL — JiM Collins

YOUR
glorious
LIFE IS
→ RIGHT HERE ←
READY to BE
chosen.

MY Shining Support

Do you have a mentor you can turn to?

Have you outgrown your mentor?

Do you have a mastermind* of people you can brainstorm with and receive advice from?

Are you using it actively enough?

Have you outgrown your mastermind*?

Do you have enough support with childcare?

*[*A mastermind is a group of people who meet—either online or in real life—to encourage and support each others' business and/or personal growth.]*

Brainstorm ways you can create or find a mastermind* that supports you:

How can you further develop with the mastermind you have?

Who is your ideal mastermind or accountability partner?

What kind of mentor(s) do you need for the next year?

Brainstorm ways you can receive more childcare support:

What do you need in order to thrive as a CEO over the next year?

Who can you go to when things suck and you just need to moan?

RECOMMENDED RESOURCES FOR SUPPORT

SELF-COMPASSION · K. Neff

The ART of EXTREME Self-CARE · C. Richardson

SIMPLE Abundance · Sarah ban Breathnach

The Millionth Circle · J.S. BOLEN

FIRST, WE Make THE Beast BEAUTIFUL · S. WILSON

THRIVE · ARIANNA Huffington

HOW TO BE A WOMAN · C. MORAN

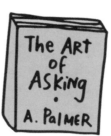

The ART of ASKING · A. PalMER

The Gifts of Imperfection · B. BROWN

YOU were
born
to be
YOU
for a very
important
reason

MY SHINING SYSTEM

It's time to check how STRONG your systems are!

First, a quick note: What do we mean when we say "SYSTEMS"?

Systems are what your business is built on. It's how things are done. Your procedures. How you run your team. What technology you use to run your business. How each task is executed.

Systems are the things that help our business grow beyond our own workload. To learn more about systems and how to create them, head to the recommended resources section at the end of this chapter!

Use this checklist to see what systems you have sorted and what you need to work on. Add your actionables to your systems notes pages at the end of this workbook to work on over the year.

By the end of the year, your systems will have grown stronger than ever to support you and your business growth!

SOPs

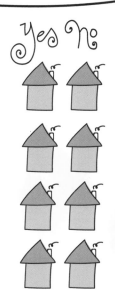

Yes No

Do you have Standard Operating Procedures (SOPs)?

Do you have a system for constantly updating your SOPs + keeping them updated?

Do you do regular reviews of your SOPs?

Are your staff trained in all your systems?

Accounting systems

Is your accounting system robust enough?

Can you easily access statistics on how much income, expenses, and taxes your business is generating?

Do you know when you need to submit tax?

Do you know what you need to do in order to submit tax?

Do you have a central place for invoices + receipts (both physical and digital)?

Is your business ready for an audit?

Organization systems

Do you have a filing system for all your digital documents, photographs + files?

Do you have a physical filing system that works?

Do you have a system for organizing + following up on all incoming snail mail?

Do you have a system for organizing + following up on all important emails?

Do you have critical documents' information backed up?

Do you have a system for making sure they are backed up regularly (i.e. monthly)?

Web systems

Yes   No

Can you easily sell your products + services using your website?

☐ ☐

Can you easily segment + talk to your mailing list?

☐ ☐

Have you reviewed all your software subscriptions + tools to see if you're paying for any that aren't helpful or aren't the right fit anymore?

☐ ☐

Are there software features you need to upgrade to?

☐ ☐

Do you have a system for making sure your computers, websites + plugins are updated to the latest version to circumvent bugs + hackers?

☐ ☐

Are you using cloud storage?

☐ ☐

Are you using a password storage app like LastPass?

☐ ☐

Legal systems

YES no

Do you have all the business registrations
you need?

Do you have the right business or company structure
set up?

Do you need an Exit Strategy?

Do you have a written plan for your business if you (or
your business partner) suffer from illness, accident, or
(gawd forbid!) death?

Does anyone else (besides you) know where that written
plan is?

Do you have all the insurances you need?

Customer systems

YES no

Do you have a system to ensure all customer support
emails + calls are answered/returned efficiently?

Are your customers taken care of beautifully in all areas
of your business?

Are you capturing customer data so you can keep in
conversation with them?

General systems

Are there places you're bursting at the seams + afraid of what growth might do to your business?

Can you build the customer experiences you want to or are you limited by your technology?

Do you have support resources in place for all critical systems?

Are there places in your business that are running on a whisper and a prayer?

Do you have systems that need to be upgraded now that you have higher volume?

Are your systems freeing you up to do what you do best?

Are you supported in the areas that are difficult or time-consuming?

RECOMMENDED RESOURCES FOR SYSTEMS

The Checklist Manifesto
A. GAWANDE

The E-MYTH Revisited
M.E. Gerber

How the Mighty Fall
J. Collins

The Entrepreneur's Trap
T. FORSYTH

The 4-HOUR WORK WEEK
T. FERRISS

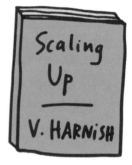
Scaling Up
V. HARNISH

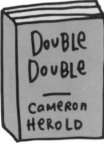
DOUBLE DOUBLE
CAMERON HEROLD

Simple Systems }

① Automate
② If you can't automate, make sure it really needs to be DONE.
③ If it needs to be done, systemate so it can easily be replicated!

MY Shining Boundaries + Balance

THIS YEAR 👁 GIVE MYSELF
PERMISSION in MY BIZ TO.

Permission slip

Taking holidays is ridonkulously important for your mental vibrance, work/life balance + your joy for life. How many holidays will you take this year?

When?

What do you need to do to make them happen?

You've got to know what YOU WANT. When you know what you want, you realize that all there is left then is

Time Management.

You'll manage your time to achieve your goals because you clearly know what you're trying to achieve in your life.

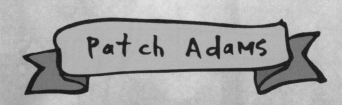

Patch Adams

WHAT *Self Care* RULES WILL I HAVE?

+ HAVE FUN COLOURING IN!!

NO WORKING AT NIGHT

NO WORK ON WEEKENDS

Adventure Saturday / Rest Sunday

GO TO BED EARLY

NO PHONES IN BEDROOM

add your own

I WILL ONLY WORK ____ HOURS A WEEK

MONTHLY SPA afternoons

READ NON-BIZ BOOKS ON WEEKENDS!

Times/Days that are WORK-FREE:

BUY + WEAR a BADGE LIKE this

get a LIFE!

I WILL LIMIT LIVE EVENTS/NETWORKING TO ONLY:

A MONTH/YEAR

Time Review

Pie Chart of
HOW YOU
CURRENTLY SPEND
YOUR BIZ
TIME →

HOW YOU
want to
spend
YOUR
BIZ TIME

WHAT ARE YOU GOING TO (STOP) DOING IN YOUR BUSINESS THIS YEAR?

Want to START creating (NEW) things, a NEW way of doing business? You need to clear out the (OLD.) You need to get rid of OLD activities, thoughts + HABits that aren't helping you move forward.

It's TIME to Stop...

INSIDE YOU THERE is the (🌱 Seed) of a Great Tree, FAR LARGER & (more) MagNIF -icent than POS SIBLY 👁 SEE RiGHt NOW.

MY Shining HABIT:

What joyful + nourishing habits would you like to cultivate? Don't worry about how hard
is to form habits—what we'll do instead is create a poster to remind ourselves each da
the beautiful things we'd like to do.

Some days we might do all of them, most days we'll only get to some . . . other days we
may not get to any of them. All of this is gorgeous + fine. It's not about perfection or fail
It's about is reminding ourselves of the toolkit of activities we have available to us.

Brainstorm what amazing habits you'd like to include + create your own poster.

 Make them sound like fun. Use words that lift you + get you excited
to do it.

 Make your habits feel achievable. On my list I say to move for 5
minutes—even though I almost always do way more. If I wrote it
down as moving for 15 minutes, it would sound like too much for
me + I would avoid it like crazy. Make it achievable so when you
do get it done, you'll feel that gorgeous sense of HURRAH + will
continue making habits happen in your day. Any extra you do will be
a bountiful bonus!

 Phrase them positively as something to move towards instead of
being a "don't."

 Copy habits that sing to you + listen to your spirit to hear what it
needs.

HABITS TO HELP ME SHINE

MY Shining Education

What do you need to learn about this year to propel you and your business forward?

What programs should you invest in?

→ → → → → → → → → → → → → → → → →

What books do you want to read this year?

→ → → → → → → → → → → → → → → → →

It's LOVE
O'CLOCK!

How much time do you need to set aside for learning and growing?

→ → → → → → → → → → → → → → → → → → → →

What training do you want your staff to have?

→ → → → → → → → → → → → → → → → → →

What do you need to do to create and support
a business that earns your income goal?

$

To Make Your dreams come true, Align Your ACTiONS WITH YOUR iNTENTIONS.

RECOMMENDED RESOURCES FOR EDUCATION

GOOD to GReat
J. Collins

Scaling Up
verne HARNISH

Delivering HAPPiNESS
.
T. HSieH

Better Than BeFoRE
G·RUBiN

The ONE MiNuTe Millionaire
M.V. Hansen
R.G. Allen

BY Invitation Only
Maybank + WiLSON

No B.S. Time Management for Entrepreneurs
D. Kennedy

SHARK TALES
Barbara Corcoran

Creating ROOM To READ
John Wood

MY Shining Customers

How could you improve your customer support this year?

Where do your customers get "stuck" the most?
What could you do to stop them from getting stuck
in the first place?

How can you reward your most loyal customers?

How can you capture more of your customers' testimonials + success stories?

Don't let the Big Overwhelm of Everything stop you from starting right now!

CUSTOMER *love* DaY

A gorgeous yearly ritual we like to do at Leonie Dawson International is our Customer Love Day, when we do something special for our customers to show them just how much we appreciate them.

You can hold a party, run a free workshop, make thank-you phone calls, send out thank you postcards, have a sale for loyal clients, or send gifts to your biggest or most loyal clients.

Consider creating a Customer Love Day for your business. Brainstorm ideas now of what you could do to celebrate the incredible tribe of people that your business serves. And schedule your own day now!

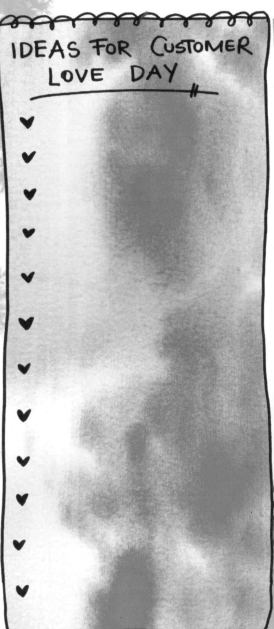

IDEAS FOR CUSTOMER LOVE DAY

WHEN? SCHEDULE IT IN!

👁 make my own dreams come true.

MY Shining Marketing

HOW MUCH DO YOU WANT YOUR AUDIENCE TO GROW IN THE NEXT YEAR?

Platform	Current #	HOW BIG DO YOU WANT IT TO BE?
Mailing list		
FaceBook		
Instagram		
YouTube		

What speaking gigs do you want to score this year?

Where would you like to get media mentions this year?

What networking events do you want to attend this year?

Testimonials: How many do you want to gather this year? How will you do this?

What will 👁 CREATE this year?

NEW!

What new products/services will you create?

How many blog posts will you create this year?

_____

A ∞ ✎ 🖍   SAVE   PUBLISH

How many newspaper articles will you submit this year? [____]

WHERE TO?

_____
_____
_____

 File Edit View Bookmarks   🔍 ☰

How many ezines or NEWSletters will you send this year?

Subscribe

What free opt-in offers will you create this year?

What other marketing goals do you want to make for your business this year?

RECOMMENDED RESOURCES FOR Marketing

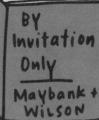

BY Invitation Only — Maybank + WILSON

Ca$h-vertising — D.E. WHITMAN

THE PSYCHOLOGY of Selling — B. Tracy

Influence — Robert CiALDINI

The Ultimate Sales Letter — D. Kennedy

SHARK TALES • Barbara Corcoran

The Entrepreneur's Guide To Getting Your Shit Together — J. CARLTON

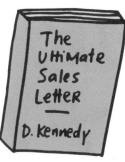

SHOW YOUR WORK! — A. Kleon

Market Yourself — TARA SWIGER

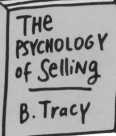

Businesses are RUN on a MOTOR of COURAGE, faith & Determination

MY Shining World

How much money do you want your business to donate this year?

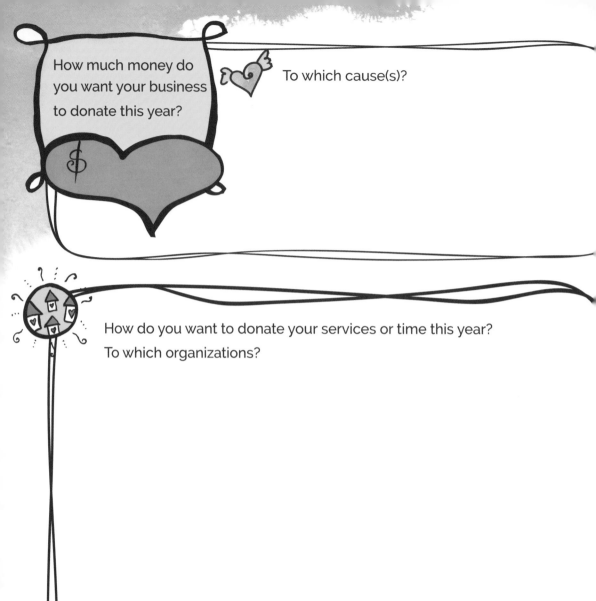

To which cause(s)?

How do you want to donate your services or time this year? To which organizations?

What ways can your business reduce its environmental impact this year?

How can your business make a positive impact on the world?

How can your business help your local community this year?

Have you undertaken the free B-Corp assessment?

B-Corp assessments help you develop a new kind of business that balances purpose and profit. The assessment will help you consider your impact on your workers, customers, suppliers, community, and the environment.

YES   NO

bcorporation.net

RECOMMENDED RESOURCES FOR COMMUNITY

The International Bank of BOB by Bob Harris

Creating ROOM to ReAD
J. Woods

White FRAGILITY • Robin DiAngelo

I'M STILL HERE • Austin Channing Brown

Braving the WilDERNESS • Brené Brown

START SomETHING that MaTTERS — B. Mycoskie

Dare To LeaD Brené BROWN

chapter ONE — Daniel Flynn

White SPACES Missing Faces C. Jackson

MY Shining Dreams

My goals that are so big and daring that
I'm not even sure they are possible are . . .

100 things to do in 2020

eam up 100 glorious goals for you to do in your business this year. Either make this
e master list of all your goals, or stretch your mind to think what else is possible. Big
small, it doesn't matter.

st get your pen writing!

1.

2.

3.

4.

5.

6.

7.

{8}

IX.

10.

11.

12.

13.

04.

15

16

17

18.

19.

20

21

22.

23

{24}

25.

26

27

28.

29.

30.

30.

32

33

34

35.

36

37

38.

39

40

41.

42

[43]

44

45

46

47.

48

49.

50.

51

52.

53.

{54.}

55.

56

57

(58)

59.

60

61.

62.

64.

65.

66.

67.

68.

69.

70.

71.

72

{73}

74

75.

[76]

77.

{78}

79.

Dream
Big
Then
Bigger!

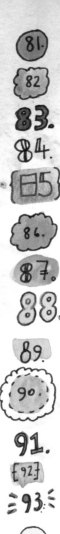

81.

82.

83.

84.

[85].

86.

87.

88.

89.

90.

91.

{92}

93.

94.

95.

96.

{97}

98.

99

100.

Dream Day

I wish this was an assignment we were given in school. I wish we'd been taught how to dream big + create the life we wanted. At least we're making up for it now, hey lovely?

I want you to write in as much DETAIL as possible your DREAM DAY. Let's talk about your dreamiest day. Where would you be? Who would you be with? What would you do?

I promise you, this is powerful! It's time to become an expert in yourself + your dreams!

Oracle Reading

I began giving myself "yearly forecast" oracle readings in 2011.

I just scrawled down the themes on a piece of paper.

It amazed me as I referred back to it each month how accurate + helpful it had been.

You can do the same—and you don't have to use oracle cards! You can use tarot, angel cards, holy texts like the Bible or Qur'an, sacred poetry books, or any other gorgeous cards or books that resonate with you.

Just sit with your intention for a few moments to receive guidance and inspiration for your coming year + begin pulling cards, or opening the text at random.

my 2011 card read... amazingly accu...

There are so many oracle + tarot cards out there that you can use. Choose the one that calls to your heart.

For a list of some of my other favorite oracle cards, head to:

www.tinyurl.com/leonietoporacles

Oracle Reading

Pull 12 oracle or tarot cards for your year ahead. If you prefer, you can also randomly choose passages from a holy book, create prayers, randomly choose lyrics, or whatever sings to your spirit! There is no wrong way to do this!

Ask your angels, guides, or God (whomever you resonate with most) to give you any messages you need to help you shine in the coming year.

If you don't have your own cards, try an online oracle . . .
I ♥ Joanna Powell Colbert at www.gaiantarot.com

Write down the card messages for each month . . .
going with the words that feel the most important.

January

February

March

April

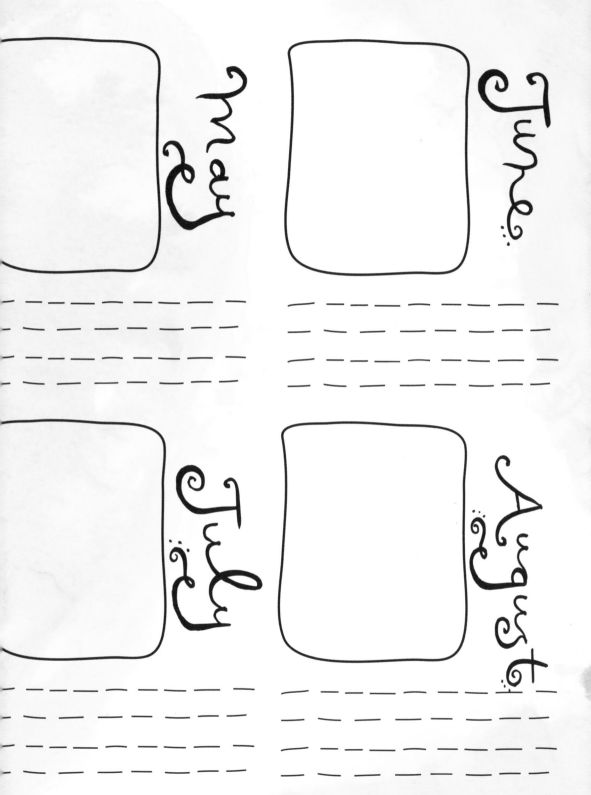

May

June

July

August

September

October

November

December

everything you are looking for is inside → YOU ←

DreamBoard

Dreamboards are an incredibly powerful tool for drawing your dreams to you through the Law of Attraction. Not only that, they serve as visual guideposts that are not only beautiful and inspiring to look at, but will help you remember every. single. day. your dreams + highest intentions for this year.

And as we all know, what we focus on becomes true. Creating your very own dreamboard right now will help seal the deal between you + your dreams!

Supplies you will need:

A piece of cardboard, thick paper or canvas in whatever size feels RIGHT To you.

Glue

SCISSORS

MAGAZINES, NEWSPAPERS, PHOTOS + IMAGES

A little blend of OPENNESS. COURAGE, JOY + A SPRINKLE OF HOPE. ☆ ♡ @ D

Search through MAGAZINES for iMages + words of things, people, experiences + feelings we'd like to draw into OUR lives for the Next year ♥ ♥ ♥

Cut out images that Lift you up, inspire you & make you feel Radiant ★ IGNORE all images + words that feel like a SHOULD.

glue them onto your CARDBOARD until it feels ⟩just RIGHT⟨ to your spirit ♥

GLUE

PLACE it SOMEWHERE YOU SEE it DAILY. ON YOUR desk, BY YOUR Bed, even on the back of your toilet door!

♥ YOU CAN ALSO USE THE FOLLOWING PAGE TO CREATE A MINI PORTABLE DREAMBOARD TO KEEP WITH YOUR WORKBOOK!

(P) You can also use PinteRest as an ONLINE dReamBoaRd. You might also Like to create a companion PinteRest Board foR dreams fulfilled too!

& watch it magically appear!

MY MINI PORTABLE
dreamboard

DreamBoard EXAMPLES

WANT TO WATCH A VIDEO NOW TOO?

www.leoniedawson.com/dreamboard

WHAT TO DO WHEN
EVERYTHING SUCK

Our feelings can change in an instant. Fickle things they are—generated by the moment, the situation, our hormones & our perspective. If we can change just one of these things, a great healing can occur.

We can go from rock bottom to, "You know what? I'm okay!" in about 15 minutes. There's a world of difference between those 2 places. All we need to do is remember the things that work for us... the little changes that can make a big difference.

Let's prepare ourselves now by writing our reminder list of Things to Do When Everything Sucks.

Cut this out + put it in a handy place (your purse or phone) in case of sucktastic emergency!

SURE! Cut me out ♥love!

In case the suckies stri

My list to de-suckify

★ go outside for 5 minutes
★ smell lavender
★ get sunshine on my face
★ eat something green
★ have a shower
★ do a 5-minute meditation or breather

MY SHINING YEAR

MAKING YOUR GOALS HAPPEN!

A goal without a plan is just a wish.

How my company turns our GOALS into ACTION

Set a DEADLINE to finish workbook

Get copies made for everyone on team ♥ ♥ ♥ ♥

PROJECT PLAN it!

LDI
Projects | Workbooks
SEND TO PRINTERS
· LEONIE | 1 March 2016
·
·

File all the goals + activities into our project management software

DRILL down to details— every single task that needs to be done to complete goal

Assign everything to WHO will do it!

Have deadlines + due dates for everything

Set QUARTERLY GOALS. Lay out BIG PROJECTS on wall planner.

2017 Planning
REVIEW | MEMBERSHIP | WORKBOOKS

REVIEW + CHECK ON PROGRESS monthly

Make your GOALS happen!

Setting your goals is just one part of the process of making things happen.

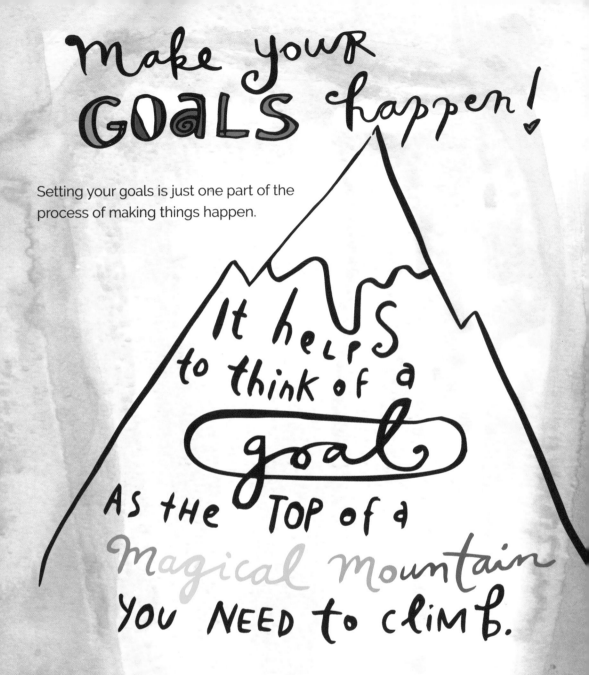

It helps to think of a **goal** AS the TOP of a *magical mountain* You NEED to climb.

Getting to the top (the goal!) is not possible with just one step!

You're going to need to climb that mountain one step at a time.

And sometimes, there will be some steps that need other things done to complete t too—which can feel overwhelming, and like the top will never be reached.

nce you have your goal, brainstorm all of the things that you need to do to get there.
st all the tiny steps that have to happen before you get to the top. Don't overthink
is! Just get them down.

SUPER tip*

If your step has more than 1
piece, separate them into 2 steps.

e really wonderful thing is this: the more you hone your steps into smaller pieces,
e more focussed you become, because the thinking is already done. You just get to
TION!

On the next 3 pages there are 3 Magical Mountains for you to fill in. Remember to bre your big items into small doable steps, and make a date to DO THEM.

REMEMBER: climbing your Magical Mountain to read your goal means doing **3** things:

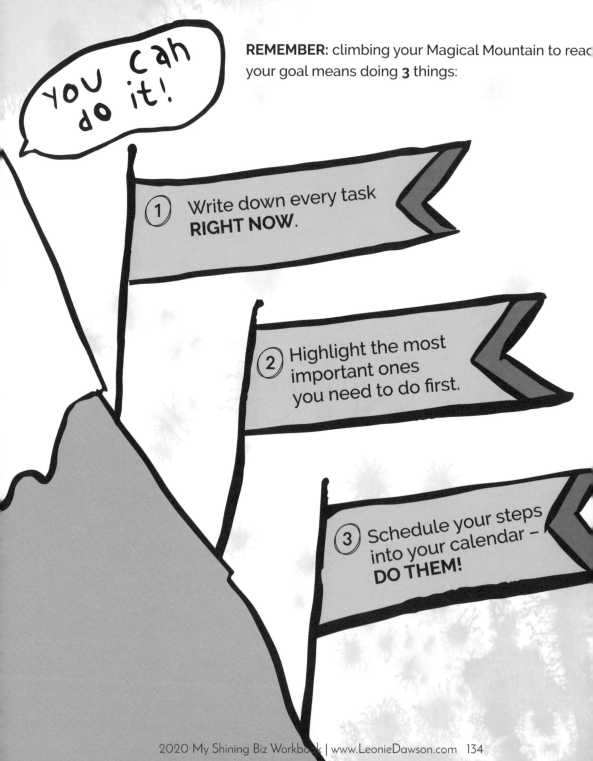

magical mountain map

ADD Project Name

Write down all the steps you need to take to get up the mountain...

& THEN NUMBER THEM! IN ORDER OF PRIORITY

What support/resources do you need

FOR THIS MAGICAL MOUNTAIN TREK?
Journal what you need here:

TIME

MONEY

HEALTH

Support

magical mountain map

ADD Project Name

Write down all the steps you need to take to get up the mountain...
& THEN NUMBER THEM! IN ORDER OF PRIORITY

What support/resources do you need

FOR THIS MAGICAL MOUNTAIN TREK?

Journal what you need here:

TIME

MONEY

HEALTH

Support

magical mountain map

ADD Project Name

Write down all the steps you need to take to get up the mountain...

& THEN NUMBER THEM! IN ORDER OF PRIORITY

What support/resources do you need

FOR THIS MAGICAL MOUNTAIN TREK?

Journal what you need here:

TIME

MONEY

HEALTH

SUPPORT

 **DON'T** **FOCUS ON** **WHAT I'M UP** against.

 **FOCUS ON** **MY** : **GOALS** +

 **try to** **ignore tHE** rest. **- VeNuS WILLiaMS**

Monthly Checkins

REMEMBER this TASTY tiDBit FROM the START of the BOOK?

It's NOT ENOUGH to just fill out this WORKBOOK + NEVER LOOK AT it AGAIN.

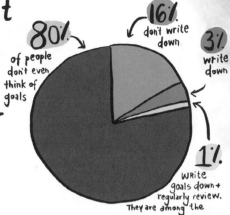

80% of people don't even think of goals

16% don't write down

3% write down

1% write goals down + regularly review. They are among the

HiGHeSt AChieveRs!

REMEMBER:

It's the 1% of the PoPuLATioN WHo WRite down theiR GoALS AND ReGulARLY Review them who ARe the HiGHeSt AChieveRs.

AND ⟨You⟩ ARe GoiNG to Be oNe of them. Have A ReCuRRiNG DATe iN YouR CALeNDAR at the StARt of eveRy MoNtH. CoMe BACk HeRe, Fill out the WoRkSHeet HeRe + Have A date with YouR dReAMS.

It will keep You on tRACk, MotivAteD + PRoductive. And You'll Be thAt iNCReDiBLe 1% of people who know How to MAke theiR dReAMS CoMe tRue.

Magic Money Maker Plan for January

HOW MUCH MONEY do YOU want to MAKE this MONTH?

HOW COULD YOU GET to that NUMBER? EXPERIMENT!

Product/Service	PRICE	# SOLD	TOTAL

What DO YOU NEED to DO to GET there?

HOW WILL YOU CELEBRATE WHEN YOU GET there?

juicy january

What Goals did You Achieve in Jan?

What WOULD You LIKE to DO Differently?

What Goals WILL YOU GO FOR IN FEB?

What DO You NEED to DO to MAKE it happen?

Magic Money Maker Plan for February

HOW MUCH MONEY DO YOU
WANT TO MAKE THIS MONTH?

HOW COULD YOU GET TO THAT NUMBER? EXPERIMENT!

Product/Service	PRICE	#SOLD	TOTAL

WHAT DO YOU NEED TO DO
to GET there?

HOW WILL YOU CELEBRATE
WHEN YOU GET THERE?

fab february

what Goals did You Achieve in FEB?

what WOULD You Like to DO Differently?

what Goals will You GO FOR iN Mar?

What DO You NEED to DO to MAKE it happen?

Magic Money Maker Plan for March

HOW MUCH MONEY do YOU want to MAKE this Month?

HOW COULD YOU Get to that NUMBER? EXPERIMENT!

Product/Service	PRICE	#SOLD	TOTAL

What DO YOU NEED to DO to Get there?

HOW WILL YOU CELEBRATE WHEN YOU Get there?

Magic March

What Goals did You Achieve in Mar?

What WOULD You LIKE to DO DifferenTly?

What Goals WILL YOU GO FOR iN APR?

What DO You NEED to Do to MAKE it happen?

Magic Money Maker Plan for April

HOW MUCH MONEY do YOU want to MAKE this MONTH?

HOW COULD YOU GET to that NUMBER? EXPERIMENT!

Product/Service	PRICE	# SOLD	TOTAL

WHAT DO YOU NEED to DO to GET there?

HOW WILL YOU CELEBRATE WHEN YOU GET there?

Amazing April

what Goals did you Achieve in APR?

what WOULD YOU LIKE to DO DifFERENTLY?

what Goals will YOU Go FOR IN MAY?

What DO YOU NEED to DO to MAKE it happen?

Magic Money Maker Plan for May

HOW MUCH MONEY do YOU want to MAKE this MONTH?

HOW COULD YOU GET to that NUMBER? EXPERIMENT!

Product/Service	PRICE	#SOLD	TOTAL

What DO YOU NEED to DO to GET there?

HOW WILL YOU CELEBRATE WHEN YOU GET there?

Marvellous May

What goals did you achieve in May?

What would you like to do differently?

What goals will you go for in Jun?

What do you need to do to make it happen?

Magic Money Maker Plan for June

HOW MUCH MONEY do you want to MAKE this month?

HOW COULD YOU GET to that NUMBER? Experiment!

Product/Service	Price	#Sold	Total

What DO YOU NEED to do to Get there?

HOW WILL YOU CELEBRATE WHEN YOU GET there?

Jubilant June

What goals did you achieve in JUN?

What would you like to do differently?

What goals will you go for in JUL?

What do you need to do to make it happen?

Magic Money Maker Plan for July

HOW MUCH MONEY do YOU
WANT to MAKE this MONTH?

HOW COULD YOU GET to that NUMBER? EXPERIMENT!

Product/Service	PRICE	#SOLD	TOTAL

WHAT DO YOU NEED to DO
to GET there?

HOW WILL YOU CELEBRATE
WHEN YOU GET there?

jumping july

What goals did you achieve in Jul?

What would you like to do differently?

What goals will you go for in Aug?

What do you need to do to make it happen?

Magic Money Maker Plan for August

HOW MUCH MONEY do YOU want to MAKE this MONTH?

HOW COULD YOU GET to that NUMBER? EXPERIMENT!

Product/Service	PRICE	# SOLD	TOTAL

What DO YOU NEED to DO to GET there?

HOW WILL YOU CELEBRATE WHEN YOU GET there?

Awesome August

What Goals did You Achieve in Aug?

What WOULD You LIKE to DO DIFFERENTLY?

What Goals will You GO FOR iN Sep?

What DO You NEED to DO to MAKE it happen?

Magic Money Maker Plan for September

HOW MUCH MONEY do you want to MAKE this Month?

HOW COULD YOU GET to that NUMBER? EXPERIMENT!

Product/Service	PRICE	# SOLD	TOTAL

What DO YOU NEED to DO to GET there?

HOW WILL YOU CELEBRATE WHEN YOU GET there?

Shining September

What Goals did You Achieve in Sep?

What WOULD YOU LIKE to DO DIFFERENTLY?

What GoaLS WILL YOU GO FOR iN Oct?

What DO You NEED to DO to MAKE it happen?

Magic Money Maker Plan for October

HOW MUCH MONEY do YOU
want to MAKE this MONTH?

HOW COULd YOU GeT to that NUMBeR? ExPeRiMeNt!

Product/Service	PRice	#SoLd	TOTAL

WhaT DO YOU NeeD to DO
to GeT there?

HOW WiLL YOU ceLeBRate
WheN YOU GeT there?

Opulent October

What Goals did You Achieve in Oct?

What WOULD You LIKE to DO DiFFERENTLY?

What Goals WILL You GO FOR iN NOV?

What DO You NEED to DO to MAKE it happen?

Magic Money Maker Plan for November

HOW MUCH MONEY do You want to MAKE this Month?

HOW COULD You GET to that NUMBER? EXPERIMENT!

Product/Service	PRICE	#SOLD	TOTAL

What DO You NEED to DO to GET there?

HOW WILL You CELEBRATE WHEN You GET there?

urTuring November

What Goals did You Achieve in Nov?

what WOULD You LIKE to DO DiFFERENtly?

What Goals will You GO FOR iN Dec?

What DO You NEED to DO to MAKE it happen?

Magic Money Maker Plan for December

HOW MUCH MONEY DO YOU
WANT TO MAKE THIS MONTH?

HOW COULD YOU GET TO THAT NUMBER? EXPERIMENT!

Product/Service	PRICE	#SOLD	TOTAL

WHAT DO YOU NEED TO DO
TO GET THERE?

HOW WILL YOU CELEBRATE
WHEN YOU GET THERE?

Divine December

what Goals did You Achieve in Dec?

what WOULD You Like to Do Differently?

Time To Review
& dream a new dream!

Grab YOUR 2021 WORKBOOKS!

What To Do

when you FALL the WORKBOOK OFF WAGON!

1.
FORGIVE YOURSELF

2.
REVIEW THIS BOOK
WHAT GOALS CAN YOU ACHIEVE THIS MONTH?

4.
GO GET YOUR GOAL, GIRL!

3.
GO PUBLIC.

TELL FRIENDS OR YOUR MASTERMIND YOUR GOAL.
ASK THEM TO HOLD YOU ACCOUNTABLE.

About the Author

Leonie Dawson is a best-selling author and serial entrepreneur. Over the past 15 years she has taught hundreds of thousands of women how to have more spirited lives and abundant businesses.

Leonie has been recognized for her business acumen by being voted a top 6 finalist in the Optus My Business Awards for Australian Businesswoman of the Year, and a finalist in the Ausmumpreneur of the Year Award. She is the current world record holder for the fastest person to build to the highest leadership rank in doTERRA.

Leonie lives on the Sunshine Coast in Australia with her husband and their two mermaid daughters.

FACEBOOK & INSTAGRAM: Leonie Dawson
WEBSITE: leoniedawson.com
WEBSITE: myshiningyear.com

MY Shining Notes

Notes, BRAINSTORMS & Delicious Doodling

notes {BRAINSTORMS} & Delicious Doodling

Notes BRAINSTORMS + Delicious Doodling

Notes, BRAINSTORMS & Delicious Doodling

notes {BRAinstorms} & Delicious Doodling

notes {BRAINSTORMS} + Delicious Doodling

notes BRAINSTORMS & Delicious Doodling

Notes {BRAINSTORMS} & Delicious Doodling

notes BRAINSTORMS & Delicious Doodling

Notes, BRAINSTORMS + Delicious Doodling

notes BRAINSTORMS + Delicious Doodling

notes BRAINSTORMS + Delicious Doodli...

notes {BRAINSTORMS} + Delicious Doodling

Notes, BRAINSTORMS & Delicious Doodling

Notes, BRAINSTORMS & Delicious Doodling

notes BRAINSTORMS + Delicious Doodling

notes BRAINSTORMS & Delicious Doodling

notes {BRAINSTORMS} + Delicious Doodling

notes BRAINSTORMS + Delicious Doodling

notes BRAINSTORMS + Delicious Doodling

Notes, BRAINSTORMS & Delicious Doodling

notes BRAINSTORMS + Delicious Doodling

Notes BRAINSTORMS + Delicious Doodling

notes BRAINSTORMS + Delicious Doodling

Notes BRAINSTORMS + Delicious Doodling

notes BRAINSTORMS + Delicious Doodling

notes BRAINSTORMS + Delicious Doodling

notes, BRAINSTORMS + Delicious Doodling

notes BRAINSTORMS + Delicious Doodling

notes **BRAINSTORMS** + Delicious Doodling